Three Wheels and Fresh Air
The Journey Continues

Eddie Loyd

Copyright © 2022 Eddie Loyd.

All rights reserved. No part of this book may be reproduced or used in any manner without the prior written permission of the copyright owner, except for the use of brief quotations in a book review.

ISBN: 979-8-9856555-0-6
(Paperback)

Cover Art by Ellen Gehring

Editing and Layout by Ellen Gehring

To request permissions, contact the publisher at beachvette79@aol.com

Printed by Lulu.com in the USA.

PRELUDE

Going through life we have different stages where we develop passions for hobbies, at a young age my first passion was playing guitar and music and in my teen years it became surfing which I continued up until 2009 and hope to get back into next year. Starting in 2007 my love of motorcycles was rekindled after riding for a few years in the early seventies. Once I bought a new motorcycle in 2007, I was ready to start exploring and this quickly became almost an obsession and it seemed like the more I rode, the more and farther I wanted to ride. I was blessed in the coming years that I saw most of this amazing country on two wheels, but in 2018 that started to change. I had some ankle surgery in the fall of 2018 and then in January of 2019 I was in a car accident and fractured my right knee. All these things plus a few motorcycle accidents and age made me decide to go to a three wheeled machine. I did not like the way a traditional trike handled going through corners and as my wife Laura had been riding a Can-Am Spyder for a few years and knew these bikes handled exceptionally well I decided to go this route. I had gone into the local Can Am dealer to take my wife's bike in for an oil change and when I walked in they had a 2019 Spyder F3T and I fell in love with it, I told David the owner of All Out Cycles do not sell this bike I will be back tomorrow to do the paperwork. From the moment I rode it home I knew and wished I had done this switch sooner; my fun level and my confidence level were sky high. I bought my Spyder in July of 2019 and went to my first bike rally in September at Delmarva bike rally in Ocean City, Maryland and went with a friend in October to ride the Tail of the Dragon in Tennessee. After this I knew I would do another cross-country trip and that is what brought me to this book. It would be two years after I bought the Spyder before I took this trip, and it was a blast and so different from riding my Harleys long distance.

This was a ride I had thought about after my trip in 2016, when I thought that might be my last cross-country trip. As time passed by, I was feeling good and even did a couple of Iron Butt Rides. I felt like I would be able to do another trip and started looking at routes I had not traveled yet and saw a few blank spots on my map that showed all the different routes I have taken.

My friends and I took a trip to Canada around the Great Lakes in 2017 and this was a fantastic trip with some of my best friends and my love Laura. Each time I did another shorter trip I started thinking even more about doing a trip for my 70th birthday. One of the sights at the top of my bucket list was Glacier National Park and the Going to the Sun Road. I started getting my road atlas out and planning different routes that would take me to this destination along with other parks and sights along the route. After many months of looking at routes I had narrowed it down to a couple of different ones and fate would sort of step in and help with the first part of the route to get to Glacier.

    As 2020 was a very trying year with the outbreak of the Covid-19 virus, which disrupted lots of vacations and holidays, by the time January 2021 rolled around everyone was hoping that the coming year would see a return to normal and I started planning in earnest to do the trip in late summer or early fall. This is where fate stepped in and really made it look as if the trip would actually happen. Our Friend Suzzette mentioned that she was going to Michigan to see our friends Tyson and Teresa in early September and asked if we wanted to join her. This would set me up perfectly to hit parts of Michigan I had not been to and put me on one of the routes I had picked for my trip to Glacier. Route 2 runs along the northern border of the United States directly into Glacier National Park and across the Upper Peninsula of Michigan of which I had only traveled a small amount of this beautiful area on our trip in 2017. I was going to call this trip the 7 for 70 ride as it would be my seventh trip across the country on my 70th birthday. We were going to Dowagiac, Michigan which was about 1000 miles from Virginia Beach which gave me a great start to the trip. I thought I might have to convince Laura to take another long trip, but she seemed excited about going and we were going to take two days to get there so it would spread the miles out. We decided we would head out on September the 10th and arrive in Michigan on the 11th, I was going to stay there for about three days then head out on my journey and Laura and Suzzette were going to stay at our friends for a few more days and then take three days to get home so they could spread the miles out a little better for them. I had my 70th birthday party in April and got quite a few gift cards and a great travel book with different sights and trivia from my daughter Ellen, which was fun trying to find most of the things she found along my projected route. Even though the route to Glacier stayed constant the ride home changed constantly and even changed daily sometimes as the trip progressed.

Day 1
The Trip Begins

As the time for departure on this adventure got closer there were so many things to get done, from getting the bikes checked out at the dealer to deciding how I wanted to pack. This was the first long trip on my Spyder, and I decided that I would only take enough clothes for about eight days and do laundry along the way. I had taken my bike in for a thorough inspection and told them if anything was border line to replace it. As the bike had about 16,000 miles, I figured that either tires or brakes were going to need to be replaced. As it turned out I needed a rear tire and front brakes, I asked about the front tires and how they felt about 7000 more miles going on them and they felt comfortable that I would be fine and as it turned it all was good and even after the trip, I still have plenty of miles left on them. The last thing you ever want on a long trip are problems that could have been prevented, especially when you are miles from nowhere. The only other decision I had to make was whether to bring my camping gear as I have tried to camp as much as possible on previous trips, but eventually decided I would just hotel it on this journey.

The morning we were leaving started as a bright sunny morning and it looked as if the weather was going to be fantastic though a little warm. We headed out from our house about 6:30 am and not long after leaving we had our first small mishap. As we were heading down the Interstate, I looked in my mirror and noticed that Suzzette was not behind Laura, so I slowed down thinking she got stuck at the light right before the expressway. As she still was not coming up, we pulled over to wait for her, after a couple of minutes I was thinking something must have happened to her and we turned around to see if we could see her. I rode all the way back to the house without finding her and was finally able to reach her on the phone. She was on the side of the Interstate and had passed us while we were waiting for her. She said her chin strap on her helmet had come loose and she was worried it would blow off. I don't know how we missed her but told her we would be back in about 10 minutes. After this little episode we had Suzzette ride between us as Laura and I had headset communication and that way if she had a problem Laura could let me know. This whole adventure set us back about a half hour and we had a good laugh about it.

The first day wasn't going to provide much in the way of sightseeing along the way but we did have a neat thing happen along the way. Once we got off the Interstate around Fredericksburg, I know I said I don't like riding Interstate but sometimes you must, we were heading North towards Winchester. We stopped in at the Marshall Diner in Marshall, Virginia which was founded in 1797 and originally called Salem. We met a couple of fellow bikers there who were getting ready to head to Delmarva bike week, which we would normally be going to if not for this trip. They were really nice guys and when they left one of the guys named Gary paid for all of our breakfast. I love small town America. Our waitress named Row was also a rider who rode sports bikes and I think we inspired her after telling her of some of our rides. We crossed the mountains of West Virginia at Sidling Gap at 1269 feet above sea level and later crossed the Eastern Continental Divide at 2610 feet above sea level. The rest of the day was spent riding some good roads to Washington Pennsylvania where we were stopping for the night. This was one of the places my daughter had found some neat things for us to check out while we were here. Once we got settled into the hotel for the night, we went to Longhorn Steakhouse for dinner before heading out to do some exploring. Laura and I headed out as Suzzette went on back to the room. Our first stop was to find the statue erected in memory of the Whiskey Rebellion of 1791. The statue honored the protesters of the first tax imposed on a domestic product during George Washington's Presidency. The tax was passed to try to reduce the war debt from the Revolutionary war. The other stop was the Pennsylvania Trolley Museum dedicated to the operation and preservation of historic trolleys. Many of the cars are from other locations and have been restored, probably one of the most famous was the car #832 built in High Point, North Carolina and used on the Desire line in New Orleans and used in the play by Tennessee Williams 'A Streetcar Named Desire'. Unfortunately, the museum had closed for the day by the time we got there. One thing we noticed while riding around downtown was the number of bars and dinner clubs they had in this small town, maybe a remnant of the Whiskey Rebellion. To end the first night on the road Laura and I went to Meadows Casino which was right by the hotel. It was a very nice casino but of course neither of us won any money and after about an hour here we headed on back to the room to get ready for another long day on the road.

Day 2
Arrival in Dowagiac
Pronounced (doe-wah-jack)

This day was not going to be very exciting, or many stops for sightseeing as we were trying to make miles to arrive at our friend's house. I know Laura and Suzzette are not used to doing four hundred plus miles a day and this would cause them to rethink their return home at the end of the week. Other than stops for fuel and lunch we rolled on through Pennsylvania, Ohio, and Michigan to arrive at the town of Dowagiac, Michigan where our friends lived. We finally arrived at about 5:30 pm after a long hot day. Dowagiac is a small town in Southwest Michigan of about 5,900 people incorporated as a city in 1877. The name of the town means "Fishing near home water" from the Potawatomi Indian tribe. The name Potawatomi means Keeper of the Sacred Fires. Once we arrived, I think we were all ready to get off the bikes, have some adult beverages and relax. We spent some time looking around their property of which they have about nine acres. It is really nice with lots of woods and trails cut all throughout and they have a four-wheeler to ride around it on. We had a nice dinner of BBQ Ribs and potatoes then spent the rest of the evening just catching up on old times as it had been a few years since we had seen Tyson and Teresa or Leadfoot as we call her. You know as bikers everyone must get a nickname. Mine is Spyderman, Laura is Brakecheck, and Suzzette is Pink, it's just part of the biker lifestyle. They had a couple of full days of sightseeing planned for us and as it had been a long hot day, we hit the sack early.

Day 3
Touring the Country Roads

We weren't going to head out seeing the local sights until about 12:00pm or so as they had to wait for a friend to come watch their dog Moxie while we were gone. As Laura and I were up early and she realized she had forgotten her pajamas, we decided to head out to Benton Harbor where there was a Kohls and to do some exploring while waiting for them. It was a nice ride of about 25 miles traveling through the rural countryside of Southern Michigan. There isn't much to do in Benton Harbor even though it is a larger city than Dowagiac but has a rather checkered past involving riots and problems with their drinking water containing too much lead. It is very close to Lake Michigan so I am sure that during the summer there are lots of outdoor and boating activities available, and I am sure that if we weren't meeting our friends, we would have found some neat things to do. Once we had gotten the pajamas, we headed back a different route which took us through lots of farmland and orchards. We stopped at one of the family orchards and bought a couple of apples fresh off the tree, they were so juicy and delicious. There are lots of lakes in this part of Michigan and we passed the Woodland Beach area, which was very pretty, we were wanting to stop for a drink and pulled into Dockside Dans which looked like a cool place, but they weren't opened yet, so we just kept rolling back to our friend's house as it was close to the time where we were going to go out on our ride together.

Our first stop was for a late lunch at the Old Tavern Inn which is one of the oldest businesses in Michigan and still in the original building built in 1835. It is in Summerville and is a biker friendly place to stop for good food and cold drinks when out riding. Our first stop after lunch was the Arthur Dodd State Park which is a fifty-one-acre park on the Dowagiac River which is a tributary of the St. Joseph River and runs thirty-one miles through the lower peninsula of Michigan. It has lots of activities available including hiking, canoeing, and tubing, this is where our friends come in the summertime for tubing, from here we went to another park which was the Russ County Park which is a 13-acre park located in the 580-acre Fred Russ Forest. There are lots of trails here for activities year-round from snowmobiling to horseback riding. Luckily there were some people bringing their horses in from a ride and as Laura loves horses, she got to pet them and get her picture taken with them. We ended the day with a stop at the Twirl Ice Cream shop in Cassopolis, Michigan on the boardwalk on Stone Lake which covers about 148 acres and is about 56 feet deep at its deepest spot. This was a place they stop at often and I had told them we definitely wanted to make a stop here especially since Laura loves her ice cream. It is a really cool place that also serves all types of food, and I am sure it is packed in the summertime. The building was originally built in 1939 and was the second Tastee Freeze in Michigan before it became the Twirl. The same family has owned it for 35 years and continue to work there to this day. Once again, we ended the day having some drinks at the house and playing some card games, another day of adventures awaited us tomorrow.

Day 4
More Back Road Riding

On the previous day I realized that I had forgotten one of my heart medications and didn't want to go almost a month without it, so I called some local pharmacies and finally worked something out. Thank goodness a CVS in Southbend, Indiana which was about 25 miles from their house, was able to get me a 30-day supply. It was pretty cool that I had a small world situation happen while there to pick it up. The Pharmacist who was helping me told me she used to visit her grandparents in Virginia Beach when she was young. They had a house right across from the Methodist Church on Pacific Avenue and that they had owned a restaurant Called Nicks. I told her I knew exactly where she was talking about and had even eaten at Nicks a few times. On the way to South Bend, which is home to the Fighting Irish of Notre Dame University, we stopped at the Rise and Shine Cafe in Niles, Michigan for a delicious breakfast, great food and awesome staff. I highly recommend this place if you are ever in the area. We had a full day of riding and sights to see. I know Teresa was excited to be riding as she had just recently gotten her motorcycle license and bought a new bike. It is always great when you become a rider instead of a passenger. We had one place where we had to make a sharp uphill turn and we thought Thersa was going to stall as she went up the hill, but she saved it and made it up through the turn. That's the kind of stuff you only learn from riding through it. The feelings of being on the open road are something that can't be described, and I am so blessed to be part of this community.

One of the main sights I had wanted to see was the Langley Covered Bridge. Covered bridges are one of my favorite sights to see other than lighthouses, especially as there are not that many left across the country anymore with about 1000 left from the roughly 12,000 there were at one time. The Langley bridge was built in 1887 and underwent major repairs in 1950, 1951 to preserve this link to a bygone era. It is 282 foot long crossing the Saint Joseph River. It is the longest of western Michigan's covered bridges and one of the longest in the nation. The Sturgis Dam is also located here and was built from 1909 to 1911 and was the first water power plant in Michigan. It is 24 foot high and 308 feet long, as far as dams go it is not very big but still generates power to this very day. One of the highlights of the day was a stop at Rawson's

King Mill Park, which is a beautifully restored mill, which has over seven acres of bridges, paths, and space for picnics. There is a beautiful dam and small waterfall and is a popular spot for photographers and for weddings. We ended up riding over 100 miles and ended the day at the Four Winds Casino where I won forty dollars.

Day 5
Hanging Out Locally

This was going to be a laid-back day just seeing some sights in Dowagiac, Laura and I headed downtown to do some shopping and picture taking as they had some cool statues scattered throughout the area, downtown also has some really great shops and we met our friends later for a nice lunch at Caruso's. One of the cool pictures we took was all of us and our bikes by the Dowagiac water tower. I hit the sack pretty early as I was heading out the next morning to start the major part of the trip. It was great seeing our friends and their hospitality was awesome, thanks to Tyson and Teresa. This was a great area of Michigan I had never visited before and much different than I had thought it would be.

Day 6
The Ride West Begins

After all the fun visiting our friends and all the great sights I was ready to start the journey toward Montana and Glacier National Park. I had packed my bike and cooler the night before so I would be ready to roll out about 5:00am, Laura was up with me to see me off. I have some neat LED lights on the front of my bike that can do multiple colors and I had them set on flash to give me more visibility. As I headed up the highway a State Trooper passed me and flipped his lights on briefly to tell me to turn them off. Each state has different laws concerning these types of lights, so I just set them to steady white. I was going to take highway 31 along the western side of Michigan with lots of amazing stops along the way towards Mackinaw City. My first stop was going to be in Holland, Michigan at the Big Red Lighthouse, which has a long history dating back to 1870 when the first structure was built. This lighthouse is Michigan's most photographed lighthouse. Lighthouses are one of my favorite sights to see and Michigan has over 100 lighthouses around its 3288 miles of shoreline, more than any other state. I remember that as my daughter was growing up, I would always tell her as she grew up that no matter what whenever you see a lighthouse beacon flashing that is my way of letting you know I am watching over you. After stopping here, I stopped at the Cherokee restaurant in Muskegon for breakfast, when I am on the road breakfast is one of my favorite meals and I love hitting the locally owned diners. Muskegon also had a 48-foot ironclad lighthouse built in 1903. There was a lighthouse just south of Sleeping Bear Dunes in Manistee, which was built in 1869 and rebuilt in 1872 after a fire destroyed the original. It is made of cast Iron and stands 39 feet tall. Many of the lighthouses along the lake are not very tall compared to a lot of the East Coast lighthouses. I love the unique styles and colors of lighthouses as each style or color lets you know which one it is along with its unique light signal.

Sleeping Bear Dunes is a National Seashore that stretches over 35 miles along the shores of Lake Michigan and at its peak rises over 450 feet about the lake. There is a lighthouse here built in 1872 and in 2011 was named one the most beautiful places in America. There is plenty of parking that brings you to the top of the dune but as you get close to the edge there is a sign that warns you that if you go down to the bottom and can't make it back up there is a minimum cost of $3000 if they have to come get you, and it could be even more if you have to be transported to a hospital. From the top of the dunes, it was amazing to see how blue the water is. There are over thirteen trails covering over one hundred miles available for hiking, skiing, and snowshoeing in the park also.

One thing I had noticed throughout Michigan were tall poles that I thought may be for growing beans but were for growing hops which are used in the brewing of beer and lots of the craft breweries buy locally. From the dunes I headed on into Mackinaw City where I would stop for the night and had visited before with friends in 2017 on our ride around the Great Lakes. Mackinaw City is a great tourist destination with access to Mackinac Island by ferry as no cars are allowed on the island. You either get around by bicycle, walking, or horse drawn carriage. I was staying at the Starlight Motel, a nice family-owned motel close to the downtown shopping area. I planned on eating at a different restaurant than last time I stayed here and had eaten at Dixies Saloon. This trip I ended up at the Rusted Spoke and sampled some of the local brews with a stone fired pizza. The view of the Mackinac Bridge from downtown is amazing, it is one of the prettiest bridges I have seen in my travels. This bridge is a suspension type bridge and opened in 1957, it is the longest main span bridge at over 26,372 foot long and rises 552 feet above the water connecting the upper and lower peninsulas of Michigan. I did some riding around town to do some shopping and bought another sticker of the Great Lakes that I had on my windshield on my previous bike, then spent some time riding around taking pictures. One sight I was on a mission to find was the giant hot dog on top of the Wienerlicious restaurant that my daughter had put in my travel book. The hot dog weighs over 3000 pounds and is 63 foot long and 12.5 feet high, if I hadn't already had dinner I would have eaten here as I love a good hotdog. I would highly recommend vacationing in the area and try to travel over to Mackinac Island at least for the day. The first day being on the road solo was a great day with lots of new sights and tomorrow would take me across the Upper peninsula which was a place on my bucket list to visit.

Day 7
Riding the Upper Peninsula Michigan

Today I would ride across route 2 which runs all the way across the UP (Upper Peninsula). I had no idea what sights I would find on this part of the journey other than a few lighthouses I had researched. Coming out of Mackinaw City you cross the Mackinac bridge to get to route 2 and head west. One of the great things about traveling solo is you can stop and sightsee whenever you find something interesting. Sometimes modern technology drives me crazy, but Google is a nice tool for finding interesting sights along the way. The morning would start off at about 49 degrees as most mornings on the trip would start off cool. Traveling this part of the peninsula the elevation would go up and down and the temperature would also, along with fog that would build in the lower areas. This stretch of highway was very rural and very beautiful. Make sure your tank is full as gas stations are few and far between along this stretch, luckily on the Spyder I have a six-gallon tank and get close to forty miles per gallon. It was about 55 miles out from Mackinaw City before I found a place to stop for breakfast, which was at the Beary Patch restaurant in Engadine, Michigan. As I was cruising along, I saw a sign for the Seul Choix lighthouse off route 431 close to Gulliver, Michigan which was about 16 miles off route 2 but looked like a beautiful lighthouse so I made the detour to visit. It was built from 1892 to 1895 and stands 78 foot 9 inches tall and the light can be seen from 17 miles away. Even if you don't want to climb the tower there are other sights to see there along with a museum. Getting there turned out to be a bit of a challenge as there was construction going on and there was a stretch of about a half mile where it was deep soft sand. This is where the Spyder came in handy and went through this stretch with no problems. If I had been on my old Harley, I would have never been able to see this lighthouse. After spending some time and getting some beautiful pictures I was off towards Manistique about 21 miles away where there was another lighthouse on the Manistique Breakwater. The light was first lit in 1916 and automated in 1969 and stands about 40 foot high. Manistique is a neat area, and I made a stop at Rapid River Knifeworks, this was a factory where they made beautiful handmade knives with handles made from all types of exotic materials and they will engrave your knife blade while you wait. I would have liked to have bought one, but they were very expensive, but

I did buy a couple of antler keychains. So far, the day was full of surprise sights with many more to come. I made a stop at the Iron Mountain Mine where you can see the tools and techniques used from 1870 to 1945, they offer a tour which takes you about 2600 feet into the mine and takes about 45 minutes. As with most trips there are always regrets over things you wish you had done, and this was one of them. I was already wishing I had set aside more days and money to be able to take the time to see things. I did get some pictures and one really cool one of the fresh mineral water coming out of the mountain and it was very cool and refreshing. The Upper Peninsula is a large body of land, and I should have allowed an extra day here also so I could visit Pictured Rocks National Seashore on the north coast of the peninsula. This may be one of the most picturesque spots in the country with lots of dramatic formations and waterfalls, oh well maybe another trip.

Continuing across the Upper Peninsula I came to the town Of Norway, Michigan which had a post office established in 1891 which in the old days gave a small town a certain status. There is quite a bit of Norse influence here and the town was named for a forest of Norway pines nearby. The town square was called Viking square and there were some nice photo opportunities here, including a statue of a giant Viking warrior. I was stopping rather often to take pictures and see the sights, such as Norway Springs well which was formed in 1903 by a 1094-foot shaft drilled by the Oliver Mining Company who were looking for iron ore. The spring has been recognized for the water's taste and won a regional tasting contest, and from April to September the locals can fill up bottles and jugs from the spring. There are not many waterfalls in Michigan, but Fumee Falls is a small 25-foot-high fall, the great thing is that it is located right beside route 2 and is easy to get to. They added a nice stairway in 2004 so you can get to the top for some nice pictures. It is an easy climb to the top so take the time to climb it.

One item I had been seeing while riding through Michigan was something called Pasties and I was determined to give them a try. As I was rolling down the highway, I saw a sign that said see the world's largest pasty, so I had to make a U-turn to stop here to see what it was all about. I went into the restaurant and asked what pasties were and was told that they are flaky pastries filled with all types of fillings from sweet fruits to different meats. The Pasty can be dated back to Cornish miners in England and were brought to this area of Michigan by the miners in the 1840's. I ordered a pepperoni and cheese, and it was very delicious and found out that the largest pasty was the one on the sign on the highway. Of course, I did get a picture standing beside it. The restaurant was called the Pasty Oven and is located on route 2 in

Quinnesec, Michigan. Also, on route 2 in Iron County is what may be the first roadside picnic area established in 1918, I love seeing as many of the highway historical markers I can stop at. I arrived in Ironwood, Michigan for the night even though I had planned on making it to Duluth, Minnesota. I got a room at the Royal Motel which is a quaint family-owned place. I had dinner at Brewster's Bar and Grill which had some unusual decorations which were different antique chainsaws hanging from the ceiling. At this point I was about 1911 miles from Virginia Beach and had been blessed with great weather so far.

Day 8
Arrival in Devils Lake

On the morning of September 17th, I was awakened about 4 am with some ferocious thunder and lightning and it was raining like crazy, and I was thinking my luck with the weather had run out. I checked my phone and the weather channel radar showed that the storm should move out of the area around 6:45 so I just laid back down for a while and hoped the weather channel was correct. I woke back up about 6:00 am and it looked as if everything was going to clear up.

Today I was heading towards Duluth, Minnesota through Superior, Wisconsin. Superior is where the Edmund Fitzgerald ore ship departed from. The ship sank in a tremendous storm just seventeen miles from port on November 10th, 1975 and was made famous in a song by Gordon Lightfoot. Duluth is a port city in Minnesota and is a hub for tourism and cargo, shipping such commodities as coal, iron ore, grain, and salt. It was incorporated in 1857 and is Minnesota's fourth largest city. One of the great tourist destinations that starts here is touring the North Shore Road which is highway 61 that takes you along the shore of Lake Superior towards Canada, this is a beautiful road that I traveled in 2017. One of the sights I tried to find that my daughter had put in my travel book was Bob Dylan's boyhood home and even with the address and GPS I could not find it, and no one could seem to tell me where it was so after a few attempts I headed on out of town. I had planned on eating breakfast at the hotel but with people still cautious with the Covid outbreak lots of them did not offer it anymore. I stopped in Ashland, Wisconsin for breakfast at the Breakwater Restaurant. The waitress was very nice and even gave me a bag of ice to put in my cooler as the ice machine at the hotel was broken. Traveling these rural roads across Wisconsin and Minnesota I saw some really cool sights, one of which was Grizz Works chainsaw carvings which opened in 1999 and is owned by Justin Howland. It is amazing work that he does with a chainsaw, and it was cool to be able to see him working on one. I also stopped at the Jacobsen Rest Area which is very close to the headwaters of the Mississippi River. It is amazing to see how small the river is at the beginning and how wide it gets as it travels 2348 miles to the Gulf of Mexico, moving goods and shipping throughout the country and is such a large part of the country's history. It is the second largest drainage system on the North American continent. After leaving the

Duluth area there wasn't much to see as far as sights as you cross into the heartland of the country and on into North Dakota. There are so many historic byways with cool names around the country and I have been blessed to have traveled many of them. I try to get pictures of the signs as I pass them but sometimes traffic or the location doesn't allow me to do that. A Lot of the roads I traveled through Wisconsin and Minnesota today were the Great River Road.

My stop for the night was going to be in Devils Lake, North Dakota. Devils Lake is a fairly small town of 7000 people, and the first house was built here in 1882. It is mostly known for being one of the best fisheries in this part of the country and the lake got its name because it is situated in a deep chasm with no visible inlet or outlet. The hotel I stopped at for the night was the Fireside Inn and the young lady at the desk was very nice and helpful. It was really cool that they provided two tickets for drinks at the hotel bar which I would use later. She directed me to a sports bar not far away named Proz Sports Bar, and I had a great dinner here and a few nice cold beers. When I arrived back at the hotel, I headed back to get my free drinks and found that it was for beer or liquor, and I mean top shelf liquor. I found out they had free food here also and tonight had been ribs. I wish I had known that before I went out, but it was all good. I did meet a fellow biker at the bar here who was from South Dakota and had ridden up to see his daughter who was a teacher at a local school, very nice people. Once you hit North Dakota and are in the plains it is mostly miles and miles of crops such as soybean, sugarbeets, and corn for grain. North Dakota is also the largest producer of honey in the nation and the second largest producer of oil. I was getting excited with anticipation that in two days I would be at Glacier National Park which is where I had set out on this journey.

Day 9
The Plains & Glasgow, Montana

This day would take me the rest of the way across the plains of North Dakota and into Montana. I think a lot of people believe that Montana is all mountains, but the eastern half of the state is a continuation of the plains from North Dakota. This is another state where you see lots of wheat and lots of oil rigs called pumpjacks getting the oil to the surface. Most of the oil from this area comes from the Bakken Formation which holds up to 18 to 24 billion barrels of crude oil and large natural gas reserves. As I arrived in Rugby, North Dakota I saw signs for the geographical center of North America, which is different from the center of the United States. This site was determined by a geological survey done in 1931 and a stone cairn that is 21 feet tall and 6 feet wide was erected. These are the kinds of off the wall sights I love to find and get pictures of. Most people traveling across this area are on the Interstate and never see these sights. It was a very small town and after some pictures at the monument I was off heading toward Glasgow, Montana. Minot is the next city you come to as you travel across North Dakota. It is the fourth largest city in the state and was founded in 1886 during the construction of the Great Northern Railway. Today it is known for the Air Force Base located close by and houses the massive B52 bombers that would fly missions from here to bomb North Vietnam during the war. I had a neat experience as I was cruising across a pretty deserted part of route 2, I saw a herd of wild horses and I wanted to get a picture of them, as I pulled over on the side of the road, they all looked up at me at the same time trying to figure what I was I guess, and it made for a great picture. The next town before I would cross into Montana was Williston which was founded in 1887 and is at the confluence of the Yellowstone and the Missouri river and located in the Bakken Formation, one of our largest oil reserves. I made a stop at the state line casino, it was a nice casino but not very crowded. I grabbed a beer which was free while you played and won ten dollars. So overall not a bad stop, a couple of free beers and ten dollars. As I was heading toward Glasgow, I traveled beside the Missouri river which runs from North Dakota to Illinois and over 2341 miles making it the longest river in North America, I had always thought that the Mississippi river was the longest. Glasgow is a small town of a little over 1200 people and was laid out in 1836 and opened a post office in 1837. There was a civil war battle fought here in 1864 that was a Confederate victory. I stayed at the Campbell Lodge and found out there was a sports bar right behind the hotel Called the Oasis. I always like when I can find a bar or restaurant very close to where I am staying. When I first walked over the door was locked and I walked back to the hotel to see if there was anywhere else to go, the clerk said they are always open so thought it was strange. I called over there and found they had another entrance, so I was able to hang out there for some drinks and dinner. The waitress was really nice and said come on back in the morning as they have a great breakfast, but I was going to be rolling out early the next morning towards East Glacier Village. I had good intentions of hitting some local bars at each night's stop and just hanging out but by the end of the day riding I was usually pretty tired at the end of the day, not as young as I used to be. LOL.

Day 10
Arrival at East Glacier Montana

Today was going to be an awesome day as I arrived at the base of the Rocky Mountains, which had a snowfall the previous night in the higher elevations. The mountains are so beautiful when they are covered in snow. It always amazes me how far away you can see the western mountains as you approach from the east. Even though I was born and raised on the East Coast and have lived close to the beach most of my life, when I get out to the western mountain areas of Montana, Wyoming, and Colorado it somehow feels like home. There is something about the beauty and the culture of the people here that is amazing. As I got close to East Glacier, I went through the town of Browning which is the only incorporated town on the Blackfeet Reservation which covers 3000 square miles, which is larger than the state of Delaware and is also the headquarters for the tribe. The tribe got their name from the dark colored moccasins that they wore. I should have looked at my maps a little better and maybe planned on staying here as it was closer to the entrance to the park, but also, I got to see some additional sights from East Glacier Village, so I guess it all worked out. As I left Glasgow I saw some large dinosaur sculptures on a hill, there was a real cool one of a Brontosaurus that I caught as the sun was coming up and it looked so real it was like something out of Jurassic Park. So many of these kinds of sights you can find on Roadsideamerica.com which is a great resource for finding the off the wall tourist sights instead of the normal things you see. This area was also famous for some of the famous western outlaws such as Kid Curry and Butch Cassidy and the Sundance kid, which I would have some more history of them later in the trip. So many of these small western towns have very nice Veteran's memorials and show the respect that middle America has for our Veterans.

As I arrived in East Glacier Village, I noticed it was a very small town and lots of places were closed for the season already, I had originally scheduled two nights here but had decided not to backtrack after riding the Going to the Sun Road and had canceled one of the nights so I would be on the other side of the mountain. I could see that during the season the village would be packed with hikers and bicyclists. As I pulled into the Whistling Swan motel there was a sign saying for check in come down to the trading post as he was down there helping them out, I love this about the small-town mentality. The gentleman at the store was telling me about a ride to the Two Medicine Lake which was about 20 miles away from the motel. The ride to the lake was so beautiful and once I got there was even more amazing. The lake is about two miles long and a half mile wide and sits between Sinopah Mountain and Rising Wolf Mountain which rises 4450 feet above the lake. If I hadn't stayed in East Glacier Village, I wouldn't have seen this beautiful spot plus the surrounding areas and the ride to the entrance to the park the next day was amazing also. There were two shops in town still open and I did a little shopping buying a Montana shirt and some jewelry for Laura. The biggest problem was finding a place to eat as the Lodge here was closing for the season tomorrow and there was a Mexican restaurant here called Serranos, so Mexican it was. They didn't open till five so I hung around outside waiting with some other people and I'm glad I was there early so I would be able to get a seat when they opened. Once they opened the doors it filled up pretty quick and I had a great meal and a couple of margaritas, but I tried to get done so they could have my table as there was a long line, there was so much food I had leftovers that I would have for lunch along the way the next day. As everything was closed by the time, I finished I headed on back to the room and would get a good night's sleep for my ride along the Going to the Sun Road which was one of my main destinations for this trip.

Day 11
Going to Sun Road

It was so beautiful waking up and seeing the sun rising on the snow-covered Rocky Mountains. Riding this road was one of the major sights on my bucket list and I couldn't believe I was finally getting to ride it. When I woke up the following morning and saw the sun coming up hitting the beautiful snow-covered Rocky Mountains, I saw that there had been more snow fall that night and gave the mountains a beautiful glow as the sun hit them. It was going to be a ride of about forty-two miles to the Saint Mary's Visitor center and the entrance to the Going to Sun Road. The Sun Road as it is sometimes called is the only road that traverses the park and is about 50 miles long, if you rode it without any stops, it would take you about two hours but there's no way you couldn't make stops to see the beautiful sights along the way. The road crosses the Continental Divide at Logan Pass which is at 6646 feet above sea level. Construction on the road was begun in 1921 and completed in 1932 with a dedication on July 15, 1933. The road is usually closed from October till June because of the roughly eighty feet of snow they get during the winter. It is one of the most beautiful roads in America with many scenic vantage points. Some of the beauty you will see are cascading waterfalls, glaciers, and towering mountains all around you as you travel the twists and turns. This road is ideal for traveling by motorcycle and really enhances the experience. If you do plan on visiting this area, check the weather conditions and try not to come much past the middle of September. I was lucky and missed the first major snowfall by two weeks and I was here on September 19th. The speeds through the park are generally slow especially if there are lots of tourists traveling, not to mention all the bicyclists and hikers you pass on the roads. Glacier was established as a National Park in 1910 and has over 25 glaciers and 200 lakes within the park boundaries, there are over 700 miles of trails throughout for hiking and skiing it is definitely an outdoor paradise.

As I entered the park this was another place, I got to use my lifetime park pass that I had bought about ten years ago and has saved me hundreds of dollars in entrance fees, even though it has gone up in price since I bought mine it is still a great deal if you travel lots. The weather starting out was a beautiful sunny morning, but some clouds and mist moved in as I climbed the mountain which created some incredible views and rainbows, even a double rainbow, one of the rainbows came down into a field right beside the road. I think this is the first time I have actually seen the end of the rainbow, and no there was no pot of gold. As I headed up toward Logan Pass the mist turned to a light snow and the temperature got quite chilly. I felt like I was stopping every few minutes to take pictures. When I arrived at the Logan Pass visitor center it was very crowded, and it was hard to find a place to park. I was surprised how crowded it was as school was back in session and it was not a holiday. Since I got back home, I have been reading about how crowded the National Parks are and many of them are only letting people in with a reservation to try to control the overcrowding. I am glad I had brought my cold weather gear as I certainly needed it up at the mountain top and would use it a couple of more times on the trip. Lake McDonald on the western side of the park is a glacial lake that is 10 miles long over a mile wide and 472 foot deep, there were lots of pullovers along the lake shore and was covered with palm size rocks worn smooth from erosion. It was at this point of the trip that I made a direction change that looking back I wish I had held to my original route, but I had miscalculated some stops and distance. I can never describe how beautiful this park is and how much it meant to finally be here, it was everything I had hoped for and a highlight of all my trips I have taken.

    As you come off the Sun Road you come into Whitefish which was first settled in 1883 and in 1890 logging crews came here to harvest the abundance of lumber in the area and the Great Northern Railroad came here in 1904 which sparked even more development. The town is now a very popular ski and hiking destination. From here is where I changed my route, I had originally planned to head down 93 toward Salmon, Idaho but knew I had already booked a hotel and the train ride in Durango, Colorado and if I took this route, I would not make it there by the 24th Of September so I stopped for the night in Kalispell, Montana and from here would decide what direction to head the next day. I could still do that route, but it would require a couple of long days on the road, and I really didn't want to be in that situation. I stopped at a Econolodge in Kalispell and decided to catch back up on my laundry while here, they had a washer and dryer here and I bought a tide pod at the front desk for fifty cents and made a nice bourbon and coke while the laundry was going, this would get me through the rest of the trip. On the way to Kalispell, I passed through Hungry Horse, and I finally made a stop for some huckleberry products. Hungry Horse is known as the huckleberry capital of the west. Huckleberries are a sweet tart berry that grows in moist mountain areas and cannot be commercially grown.

I stopped at the Huckleberry Patch, and they had all kinds of products and gifts. I bought a jar of jam and a neat metal sign to hang on my backyard fence, and then saw they had a restaurant and bought a slice of huckleberry pie with a scoop of vanilla ice cream, it was so delicious. This day has been one of the best days of all my trips and I feel so blessed to be able to do what I have done. Sometimes I can't believe that I have traveled all over this magnificent country. That night as I looked at my maps and options, I decided to change my route and head toward Bozeman the next day.

Day 12
Bozeman, Montana

Heading out this morning it was a pretty cold morning, and I couldn't wait to find a place to stop for breakfast and a cup of coffee. I stopped at the Echo Lake Cafe which is an iconic restaurant in Bigfork, Montana that has been open since 1960. Most of their juices and pastries are made fresh and they even smoke their own salmon for their salmon benedict. I thought about trying this but I'm not big on fish for breakfast. After a great breakfast I would pass Swan Lake which is a popular spot for fishing, hiking, and skiing and began as a logging community in the early 1900's to harvest lumber for the railroad being built. I would ride past some more incredible scenery and mountain ranges. The Mission Mountains are stunning, rising to a height of 9820 feet and they were covered with snow. Today's ride was a relatively short ride of 291 miles but very beautiful, with lots of snow-covered mountains and some very unique sculptures of dinosaurs along the way. Also, along route 12 outside Helena at McDonald Pass there was one of the springs that are available in Montana where you can pull over and gather fresh water coming out of the mountain. I saw lots of people stopping to fill up jugs as I filled my drinking bottle. I would be traveling down a long stretch of the Rocky Mountains and I had decided to head toward Bozeman, Montana for the night as this was a town I had never visited, and it looked like a neat place to hang out for the night. I made a beer stop at the Big Bull Bar and Grill in Winston, Montana not far outside Helena which is the capital of Montana. A unique place close to Three Forks off highway 287 was the Bleu Horses which are 39 horses sculpted from steel scattered over a hillside completed in 2013. The name is taken from a color of horse called a blue roan and created by Jim Dolan. As I approached them, I thought it was a herd of horses but realized they were not moving, it was a great photo opportunity.

Bozeman is a really cool town with an awesome downtown area. Bozeman was founded in 1864 and named after John Bozeman who established the Bozeman trail. The Northern Pacific Railroad reached Bozeman from the east in 1883, and the first post office was built in 1915 and the building was once used in the film A River Runs Through it starring Brad Pitt. Even though Bozeman is the fourth largest city in the state with a growing population it still has that small town western feel to it, with some great shopping and restaurants and a thriving downtown area. I ended up at the Crystal Bar for some drinks and dinner at the Rocking R Bar where I had a burger made from local Montana beef from the Wagyu Cattle company, which was incredibly tasty. I spent a fair amount of time downtown going into the different shops. I was staying at the Royal 7 motel about three blocks from the downtown area, which was very convenient and reasonably priced. This is another town that if I had not already booked some events for later in the week, I would have spent an extra day here. Part of the next day would take me through some areas I had traveled before, but I would see some different sights that I had not previously.

Day 13
Yellowstone & Jackson, Wyoming

Heading out of Bozeman today I would travel down route 191 to the western gateway to Yellowstone National Park, which I have visited a couple of times before but as I was right here, I figured I would ride through again and look for some new sights. I will be traveling through some of the most unique ecosystems and beauty in the world today. On March 1, 1872, Yellowstone became the first national park in the United States and is considered by many to be the first National Park in the world. The park is known for its diverse wildlife and its many geothermal features with Old Faithful being one of the most popular. The park covers an area of over 3,468 square miles comprising lakes, canyons, and mountains. With Yellowstone Lake being one of the highest elevation lakes in North America and over half the world's geysers are in the park. Seeing the steaming cauldrons and pools of turquoise water bubbling is an amazing sight and it feels as if the earth is about to explode at any moment. Old Faithful is one of the most visited sites in the country. The geyser got its name in 1870 and was the first geyser to be named. It is fairly predictable and has erupted every 44 minutes to two hours since 2000. The water will shoot from ninety to one hundred twenty-five feet into the air and last about 15 to 20 minutes. There is a huge circle of concrete around the geyser where tourists will start gathering to see this incredible display of nature. Yellowstone is such a large park and has over 251 miles of roads so it makes it very hard to try to see it in one day, if you can get reservations there are nine lodging facilities with over 2000 rooms which seems like a lot, but they fill up fast, there are also 12 campgrounds with over 2000 sites available. I have traveled a couple of the loops and wanted to try one of the other loops, but the park was unbelievably crowded as it was the middle of the week in September, so I just traveled some of the side roads off the main loop that would take me to the south entrance. The west entrance is probably the most developed area outside the park with lots of hotels and souvenir shops but very commercialized, not the kind of things that appeal to me being so close to so much beauty. Thank God the Government has preserved this land for future generations. One of the parking areas where I stopped to walk around was right beside a river where lots of people were fly fishing. This is something I really wanted to try, it just looks so cool to see them standing in the middle of a river with waders on and gently flicking the lures into the river with such grace. It is amazing to see some of the lures that people tie themselves, they are like works of art.

As you head out of the south entrance you come into the Grand Teton National Park and the Bridger Teton National Forest. The Tetons are one of the most beautiful mountain chains in the country and my personal favorite. Grand Teton Park is only 10 miles south of Yellowstone but is connected by the park service managed Rockefeller Parkway. Grand Teton Park is approximately 310,000 acres including the major ranges of the Teton Range. The three protected areas combined cover over 18 million acres of the Greater Yellowstone Ecosystem. At 13,775 feet Grand Teton rises 7,000 feet above Jackson Hole. The three main peaks are known as the Three Sisters and are such a prominent sight to behold. There are over 1000 campsites available and over 200 miles of trails to be enjoyed. There are a few western themed lodges to stay in the park but are very pricey, but if you want to see a spectacular sunset stop at the bar at Jenny Lake Lodge and have dinner or a drink and watch the display of nature at its best.

Jackson, Wyoming lots of time called Jackson Hole gets its name from the valley it is located in and is a popular tourist area due to its proximity to three ski resorts as well as Yellowstone. Jackson was named in 1894 and incorporated in 1914. A few of the early buildings can still be found throughout the unique town square. One of the neat parts of their history is they elected the first all-woman city government which was highly unusual for those days. The town square or George Washington Memorial Park in Jackson is one of the most unique I have seen in my travels around this amazing country. At each of the four corners are arches made from elk antlers, the first one was constructed in 1953. The antlers are gathered up by the boy scouts where the elk come into the valley at the elk refuge for the winter. Each arch weighs about 14,000 pounds. The square is a hub for lots of activities in town and they also stage old western style shootouts here. I had stayed in Jackson about seventeen years ago while on a wagon train ride and it had been a great place to stay. It is still a great destination but like lots of things its popularity has caused a huge influx of tourists and residents and the hotels have gotten very expensive. I stayed at the Virginian Lodge which opened in 1965 and is a large lodging complex with rooms and RV sites, the bar and restaurant were closed as the hotel had recently been sold after the original owner passed away and is undergoing renovation. While waiting for my room to be cleaned I went over to Eleanor's Again, a bar beside the hotel that is connected to a liquor store. One of the great places to hang out at the square is the

Million Dollar Cowboy Bar, it got its name after the owner remodeled the old bar and insured it for one million dollars. The original bar opened in 1937 and has been a popular watering hole for decades. Along the main bar the stools are actually saddles which look really neat and a must to get your picture taken here but are not really comfortable. I had a really cool small world story while having a drink here. I had posted a picture sitting on one of the saddle bar stools and a friend in Florida sent me a message telling me about a friend she had in Jackson that worked across the square. I walked over to the retail store and asked if there was someone named Amy here, well you can imagine the look on her face not having a clue who I was. She answered yes, that's me who's asking, and I said a friend named Maureen said to come ask for you and she was like oh my god you know Mo, here in Virginia we call her Bunky. She was so surprised, and it was cool to meet someone that has a friend from home. Today was an awesome day with great adventures even with traveling through some areas I had been through before, and tomorrow would take me to new areas of the country.

Day 14
Road to Grand Junction

Today would be an amazing ride of previous sights and some new roads thrown in, it started off a pretty chilly morning especially going through the mountains on highway 191 toward Pinedale, Wyoming. I passed pretty close to Gannett Peak which at 13,804 feet is the highest point in Wyoming. I was ready to make a stop for breakfast and warm up and stopped for breakfast at the Wrangler Cafe in Pinedale, Wyoming and filled up on some delicious biscuits and gravy. Pinedale is a quaint little town that is located close to the Wind River mountains and is a destination for hunters, there is also the Museum of the Mountain Men here and over 1300 lakes in the area. About halfway between Jackson and Pinedale I made a stop at a little store at Rim Station to grab a cup of coffee and warm up some and had one of those neat experiences you have on the back roads. I started talking to the guy running the store who looked like a western cowboy and getting a few good stories from him. He was telling me that he owns a ranch in the area of about 10,000 acres which on the East Coast would be huge, but he said his other rancher friends gave him a hard time saying his ranch was like their front yard, as lots of these people have ranches that measure 100 square miles, it is hard to imagine that much land. His name was Brent and was a super nice guy, he told me during winter they might get over fifty feet of snow, and in Virginia Beach we are lucky if we get a couple of inches.

My next stop would be at the Flaming Gorge National Recreation area, a place I had visited before but was worth seeing again. Along the way to the gorge, I would pass lots of signs of the old Oregon Train and the path the Pony Express passed. It is amazing to still see the ruts from the wagon trains that passed this way on their way west. The Oregon Trail was over 2170 miles long going from Missouri to Oregon, I can't imagine packing everything and heading west not knowing where or what you were in for. These early settlers were tough brave people, it is estimated that over 20,000 people died making this journey. The Pony Express also traveled this area getting the mail and packages delivered from Missouri to California before the train lines were built. It only operated from April of 1860 to October of 1861. Most of the riders were very young and runaways and orphans and despite the harsh conditions they worked in only seven documented deaths happened.

Next stop Flaming Gorge is known as the Art Gallery of Time, which runs through the states of Wyoming and Utah and was discovered by John Powell in 1869 and got its name from the red sandstone cliffs. The centerpiece is the 91-mile reservoir created in 1964 by the damming of the Green River. It is a hydroelectric dam and is also popular for boating, hiking, and rafting. There are two roads that go around the gorge, route 191 and route 530 and will give you two different perspectives of how it looks. Going down 191 takes you across the dam which was started in 1958 and finished in 1964 and holds almost four-million-acre feet of water. There is a visitor center there which tells you about the construction of the dam. Crossing the dam on 191 will take you down toward Vernal, Utah. In this part of the country there were dinosaur displays and museums in every little town or crossroads. You could see the effects of the drought out west as lots of the lake's water levels were way down. I traveled lots of miles on the Dinosaur Diamond byway where my granddaughter got a kick out of the pictures of all the different dinosaurs along the way. This is another area where there are huge oil deposits with an estimated 275 million barrels of crude. I crossed into Colorado in the town of Dinosaur, which is the gateway to Dinosaur National Monument one of the cool things I saw along route 139 close to where I crossed Douglas Pass at 8268 feet was as I was cruising along I noticed a herd of mule door grazing on the side of the road and I slowed down and about five or six of them just walked across the road in front of me and I got a great picture of them. I love nature. Also saw some buffalo which are always cool to see as they are such a majestic animal. It is hard to believe how the buffalo had been killed almost to extinction and at one time there were between 50 to 60 million roaming the prairies of the United States. The plains Indians would always use everything from the buffalo and never waste them but the pioneers and people building the railroads would just slaughter them and leave the carcass to rot. I was going to stay in Grand Junction where I had stayed before in 2012 and I actually stayed at the Balanced Rock hotel with my friend John. They had new owners who had taken over the month previously who were very nice people and were remodeling the hotel. It was a very convenient place close to plenty of restaurants. John and I had eaten at a pizza place back in 2012 that was close to the hotel, but it had gone out of business. I ended up just grabbing a sub using one of my gift cards I got for my birthday and hung out in the room as it had been about an eleven-hour day due to all the stopping I did for pictures along the way. Today had been a great ride and as always, a way to feel the freedom of the road and the beauty of the country.

Day 15
Mesa Verde & Durango

    Today would be an incredible day with so much new territory and sights to see that have been on my bucket list, but today would also provide one of the disappointments of the trip. I was going to head west for a few miles before heading south toward Four Corners. Route 191 would take me down towards Arches National Park which I had always wanted to see but when I arrived there the park was full, and they weren't allowing any more visitors into the park and said to come back in three hours or so but that was not an option for me as I had miles to travel. This was another example of where all these people were coming from in the middle of September which should be off season. Maybe I will get back out this way again, who knows, maybe do an 8 for 80 trip in 2031. Another stop on my bucket list was the Four Corners monument at the corners of New Mexico, Arizona, Colorado, and Utah. It is the only place where four states share the boundary. It is also the boundary for the Navajo Nation and the Ute Tribe. It is located about 20 miles off route 160 and is maintained by the Navajo Nation parks and recreation bureau. People have been coming here since 1908 to get their pictures taken at the disk placed there, there are vendors set up around the monument selling Indian souvenirs and artifacts, there is a small admission fee to get in, but it was only five dollars. It was neat to finally see it, but it wasn't quite what I thought it would be but still cool to say I have been there.
    Rolling on from here I was headed to Mesa Verde National Park which was an incredible sight to see and a place you could spend a couple of days seeing all the sights and exhibits here. The park is a Unesco world heritage site and holds some of the best preserved Puebloian archeological sites. The area has been a National Park since 1906 and dates back as far as 7500 BC and the ruins from about 750 AD. I stopped to visit as many of the ruins as I could, but you could spend so much time here and from the highway it was about a 25-mile ride up through the mountain to get to the ruin area, but I must say the ride was amazing with lots of twists and turns. When I first arrived at the entrance to the park and found out that it was about 25 miles to the top and where the ruins were I almost didn't do it, as I knew I needed to arrive in Durango that evening. It amazes me when I see things that have been built in the past and wonder how people accomplished what

they did with very rudimentary tools and locations in the middle of nowhere. The early locations they inhabited were basically pits in the ground but even these were engineered with practicality in mind, but to see the dwellings carved into the sides of the cliffs and the detail that they had was inspiring. I can't imagine doing this with basically sticks and stones hanging off the side of a cliff. The Cliff Palace is the most amazing and was believed to be a place of high social and ceremonial use. The early inhabitants moved from their basic dwellings to build the cliff dwellings to afford greater protection. The drive up and back was so worth it, and I am glad I decided to do it and I still arrived in Durango by about 6:30pm.

Durango is a small city in southwest Colorado with a great past connected to the growth of the country and early mining of minerals. This was one spot I had wanted to visit and had actually been close to on previous trips but had not been able to work it into the route, but on this trip was planned as one of the primary spots even though a little mis planning had caused me some time issues. I was staying at the Siesta Inn which was about two miles outside the center of town. It is a nice family-owned motel very clean with a cool vibe to it. The famous cactus sign has become a landmark of Durango and is reminiscent of the motels on old Route 66. They have a really nice firepit in the common area of the motel and lots of people hang out there relaxing, talking, and having a cold beverage. I was going to ride back downtown but some other bikers there said to hop on the bus as parking can be a bear sometimes and the bus is only fifty cents for us old-timers. Turned out to be a good decision and then I could relax and not worry about driving around town. The bus dropped me off right on main street and I went looking for a place to eat and saw a sign for the El Ranch Tavern and headed on in. As I was ordering a drink, I asked for a menu, but the bartender said it was just a bar and served no food. Well, I had a couple of drinks here and chatted with a guy named Marco and he was telling me about different places to eat. Some of the best food he was telling me was at the food truck area most located at the 11th street station which from the 1920's till the 70s was mainly a place for auto repair shops and such but now there are seven food trucks here. Marco told me that there was a place that had an awesome crab cake wrap but being from the east coast I am pretty particular about my crab cakes, but he said he was from New Jersey and knows crab cakes. This was another bar I should have come back to and hung out as they had entertainment and Marco said I could hang with him and his friends. I decided to walk around and see what else there was, I stopped in to the Old Tymers cafe which has been around since 1981 and is a local's favorite and I tried the Rodeo burger which was amazing. A couple of guys sat down at the bar, and we started talking as one of the guy's named Gene is also a rider. He was telling me how he and his son wanted to do some long trips together and I told him to find the time to get it done and not have regrets about not getting it done. When I told him I was 70 he was like damn I'm 58 and I look older than you do, which I always find comical, and I got a picture with him. It seems Durango keeps causing me some minor regrets and I should have stayed downtown as there are lots of bars and breweries located downtown, but today had been a really long day and I knew tomorrow would be also but would also knock off another item on my bucket list.

Day 16
Silverton Durango Railroad

This day was going to be a highlight of the trip as it was something I had wanted to ride for years. The Durango Silverton Railroad is one of the most famous and one of the few remaining narrow gauge railroads in existence. The line was constructed by the Denver and Rio Grande Railway in 1881 to 1882 with a goal of reaching the mineral riches in Silverton, which is deep in the San Juan Mountains. The railroads were exploding across the west to bring pioneers and to mine and transport the abundance of different minerals found in the western states. There are huge silver deposits in this area, but the mountains and isolation can make it very difficult to get the ore to the smelters. I could write a whole book about this railroad and there are many different ones available. I would recommend the official guidebook of the Americas Railroad. It is very informative and has lots of pictures which show the beauty of the mountains as the Train travels approximately 47 miles to Silverton. I had booked my trip back in July and I do wish that I had made it for a couple of days later so that I could travel the longer route to get to Durango but once it was booked, I was locked into those dates plus the season was coming to an end as they shut down the line all the way to Silverton due to the heavy snowfall. They have numerous styles of cars available from completely closed luxury cars to open cars. I rode in the Silver Vista, which is open window style with a clear top, so you get a full view of the scenery as you cruise along. This trip is about a ten-hour round trip to Silverton and back, so it is a full day.

The line uses some diesel locomotives but also some of the original steam locomotives which were pulling us on this day, it just seemed the way to do it on such a classic line. I arrived at the depot in downtown Durango about 7:30 even though the train didn't leave till 9:00 am. There is a great gift shop located here and a museum housing many artifacts from the history of the line. Each car has its own personal attendant that provides you with anything you need on the ride, which includes a full bar and blankets if you get cold. It was pretty cool that when I got on there was a nice travel bag and drink mug in my seat, so it was a nice souvenir. We had a great guy named Henry in our car who took great care of us on the trip. Not long after leaving the depot they served us a nice fresh muffin made at a local bakery and they told us about gifts that were available on the train, from CD's to books. I bought one of the books which was very informative about the history of the railroad. The scenery was amazing traveling along the Animas River in an old-fashioned steam locomotive. The Animas River is a 126-mile-long river which is a tributary of the San Juan River which is part of the Colorado River System. The river is a powerful river with rapids and pools where you can fly fish, even though you are not supposed to eat the fish as there is still arsenic runoff from the silver mining through the years. As you ride the rails you will notice a blue tint to the river which comes from the chemicals. Silverton is a National Historic Landmark and part of the San Juan Skyway with the Million Dollar Highway running from Silverton to Ouray. This highway which is route 550 is about 305 miles in total and was built in 1926 and is one of the most beautiful rides of any route in the country, and probably is one of my top five routes I have traveled. The million-dollar part of the route is about 25 miles long and got its name as it cost about a million dollars a mile to build. Silverton is still a difficult isolated place to reach, and I can't imagine what it was like in the 1800's. The first house was built in Silverton in 1874 and would slowly grow until 1882 when the rail link to Durango opened up and in the 1880's the small town boomed with the riches in silver in the mountains. Silverton was a wild wide open western town with many saloons, prostitution, and gambling. Like most towns based on mining Silverton had plenty of ups and downs according to the ore markets. World War 2 saw an increase in mining operations but by war's end depleted supplies of ore and environmental concerns pretty much spelled the end for mining, but Silverton was making a transition to a tourist economy. With the beautiful mountains and valleys in the area along with the railroad it became a destination for hiking, fishing, rafting and is the only town in San Juan County and remains an authentic frontier town and one of the west most interesting locations.

 Due to the elevation change from 6500 feet in Durango to 9300 at Silverton it requires two of the steam engines to get to Silverton but only one on the return trip. There is one section at a bridge where they must disconnect one engine to cross the bridge due to the weight and then reconnect to finish the journey. The train makes one stop on the way to fill the boiler with water which requires about 5000 gallons of water to make the steam to drive the wheels. Seeing these huge engines is a marvel of engineering and power. The current engines use recycled oil to fire the boilers instead of coal to reduce the fire risk from the embers that would come out of the stack. It was pretty cool being able to enjoy some cold beers as we wound our way toward Silverton, sometimes with the train right at the edge of the cliffs with the Animas River hundreds of feet below. Sometimes on some of the sharp turns you can get great pictures of the engine as it pulls up the steep grade, there was one section where the rocks of the gorge are a hand's length away from the side of the train. and you would be wise not to stick your hands or head out past the window. The train makes one stop along the way for hikers and backpackers to access the Chicago basin which attracts about 100,000 hikers a year. I would advise being in good shape if you are planning on hiking this rough terrain. This area is pretty famous in the movies also as it was used in parts of "Butch Cassidy and the Sundance Kid" and the scene where they jumped off the cliff, Around the World in Eighty Days was also partially filmed here. Once you reach Silverton you will have about an hour to two hours to look around the small mining town. There are restaurants and shops here, but the restaurants can be crowded. I grabbed some pizza at the Golden Block Brewery where I had eaten back in 2016 that has great brick fired pizza and fresh brewed beers and I ended up with leftovers which I would eat along the way the following day. We had a small glitch on the way to Silverton with the engine, so we only had about an hour in town so by the time I had lunch it didn't give me much time for shopping, but I did find some nice jewelry for my wife Laura for our upcoming tenth anniversary. When you hear the train whistle blow to board you best not waste any time as it pulls out on time, and it would be a long hike back to Durango. There is only one main street in Silverton as the permanent population is currently about 599 residents and only a few hotels in town. The train ride back to Durango takes about the same amount of time but it is cool seeing the scenery from the return perspective. If you are ever in this part of Colorado, I would highly recommend spending some time here and taking this ride through history. It was more than I ever thought it could be and not only historical but beautiful. We arrived back in Durango about 6:00pm and here is where I wish I had stayed another day here with all there is to do here. As much as I love being home I always hate when a trip starts the homeward leg, I just love being on the open road and seeing new sights and meeting new people. Riding the highways is truly a passion that I can't describe, and I wish everyone could experience what I have through the years.

Day 17
Back into the Prairie

Well after an amazing nine days in the Rocky Mountains I would cross the Continental Divide at Wolf Creek Pass, which is at an elevation of 10,856 feet, only this time I will be heading east toward Lamar, Colorado. Wolf Creek Pass is a pretty steep grade of about 6% and was made famous in a C.W. Mccall's song called Wolf Creek Pass which is about a runaway truck. As you come down the eastern side of Wolf Creek Pass you begin coming back into the great plains which is a drastic difference from the Rocky Mountains. Before I arrived at the pass, I was searching for a place to grab some breakfast and came across a place in Pagosa Spring, Colorado called 2 Chicks and a Hippie, it was a happening place with really good food and homemade pastries if you ever pass this way stop in and check out the decor, was a really neat stop.

Lamar is a town in eastern Colorado at an elevation of 3,619 feet which is about 7,000 feet lower than Wolf Creek Pass. As you are heading across route 160 you are in a valley with numerous beautiful mountain ranges such as Spanish Peaks and route 160 is known as the Scenic Highway of Legends. One of the weird but cool things that happened on this stretch of the trip was as I was riding along, I noticed some yellow butterflies all around me and as I kept going there became more and more of them and before to many miles, they were everywhere like a migrating swarm of them, which I found that there are many types of butterflies that migrate through this area and some swarms so large they show up on radar. They were so thick they were hitting me and my bike and splattering everywhere, I must say they were rather juicy. By the time I got through this swarm and stopped for gas I had to clean my windshield and my radiator which was covered with them. I believe that the ones I ran into were called the Clouded Sulphur which migrate from the northern parts of the country to Florida during the winter months. While I was getting gas and cleaning the bike and myself a guy at the station asked me which way I was heading and he said I may see what is known as the tarantula migration, which in fact is actually the male tarantulas looking for the females that are in their burrows. It would have been sort of cool to see this but could be rather creepy also. Even though my road name is Spyderman I am not particularly fond of spiders. I was going to stay at the Golden Arrow motel on this night, it was an older motel and was under new management and undergoing remodeling. Even with all that going on it was a clean comfortable motel. Lamar is a pretty small town and as I drove through town, I didn't see many places open. I asked the people at the front desk, and they suggested a place called the Buzzards Roost which looked like a cool place, but it was closed, so I decided to ride around for a bit and saw a Mexican restaurant but when I walked up to the door it was closed also but there was a lady inside cleaning, and she told me there was another Mexican restaurant just outside of town call La Mission Villanneva which was open. I ordered 32 oz. margarita which was huge and very tasty along with a shrimp quesadilla which was also huge and would serve as lunch the next day. I was hoping there would be a bar open somewhere but there didn't seem to be, so it was another early night. It is so much different riding the straight roads of the plains than the mountains and if you pull over it is like you can see forever and I get some great photos of what I call the Lonely Roads and I have an Instagram page called Lonely Road Photos, check it out sometime.

Day 18
Dodge City & Salina Kansas

    Kansas is a state I used to dislike having to ride across but since my first trip which was hot and windy as hell, I have found new things to explore and like about the plains state. Today's route would take me through one of the most famous towns in western history which is Dodge City. The television show Gunsmoke was based on this wild west town and the famous Long Branch Saloon which Miss Kitty Owned, even though it was about fictional characters, people my age grew up with Marshall Matt Dillion and his exploits. I had been through Dodge City in 2012 with my friend John but after nine years it was time to check it out again. Fort Dodge was established in 1865 to protect the settlers traveling the Santa Fe Trail from Indian attacks. In August of 1872 a group of businessmen organized the Dodge City town company and was originally called Buffalo City. The town developed a reputation for being the most wicked town in the old west and such notorious characters as Wyatt Earp, Doc Holliday, and Big Nose Kate either lived or visited here. So many people died in fights and the gunfighters dying with their boots on they developed the Boot Hill Cemetery which was used until 1878. One neat thing I learned about Boot Hill and why they buried people on a hill was because they used wooden coffins and by burying on a hill it allowed water to run off and not rot the coffins as fast. At one time Dodge City was the buffalo capital of the west but by 1876 so many buffalo had been killed they were almost extinct. Dodge was a lawless city and out of control until Wyatt Earp, Bat Masterson and their brothers brought law and order to the city. By 1886 with the trains running this eliminated traffic on the Santa Fe Trail and with the cattle drives using the rails the outlaw period dried up and now only a small section of town preserves the memory and artifacts of this bygone era of western history. As you travel towards Dodge City you will find scenic turnouts that tell you about the Santa Fe Trail and how important it was to the growth of the country's western expansion. It still amazes me to see the wagon ruts and to think how many people and wagons traveled this area for the ruts to still be visible. The Boot hill Museum is a neat place to visit that is a reproduction of what main street Dodge would have looked like back in the day and is located at the site of the original Boot Hill Cemetery and contains about 200 guns from some of the famous gunfighters and marshals and over 200,000 other artifacts of the wild west. While you are here stop in and have a cold beer or sarsaparilla at the Long Branch Saloon, the original Long Branch was destroyed by a fire in 1885. If you visit the museum during the summer months you will see reenactments of good old gun fights. It is definitely a cool place to visit, especially if you like history as much as I do. Other than visiting Boot Hill again I headed on out of Dodge then made a lunch break at a rest area and had my leftover quesadilla.

There is lots of windmill power going up in this part of the country as the wind almost never stops blowing. The windmills are supposed to be a clean way to generate power, but there are always repercussions no matter what may be used to generate electricity. The larger turbines can require up to sixty gallons of oil in the housings and the manufacturing process of the giant blades consumes lots of energy, not to mention disposal of the blades at the end of their twenty year life span. I saw lots of the blades being transported by rail which requires one and a half flat cars for each blade and seeing the tractor trailers moving them to the install site. You don't realize how huge these blades are until you see them going down the highway. I saw one going up an on ramp on the highway and it was quite a feat of driving to get it done. I admire truck drivers and what they do to get goods transported all across the country. I guess seeing them out west they are like a modern day cowboy. Around Spearville there was a large windmill facility and they had a cool roadside display showing the generating capacity of windmills nationwide and how they work, it was pretty informative. As the prairie is very flat, I found a place called Pawnee Rock which at one time stood over 150 foot tall but today is about 50 feet as much of it was used to build the railroads. In the early days it was a meeting place for the various Indian tribes in the area and many battles were fought here through the years. It was about halfway on the Santa Fe Trail and was a landmark plus it gave a great view of the distant plains and is covered with names of the people who passed it. Today was a pretty warm day and I found a place to stop for an ice cream in Kinsley, Kansas and of course I had to send Laura a picture as I know how much she loves her ice cream stops. I got checked into an Econo Lodge in Salina, Kansas and being in Kansas I wanted a great local Kansas steak. Too bad so many people that work at hotels know nothing about the area they live in. I asked the young lady where I could get a good steak and her response was Lone Star Steakhouse, while they do have good steaks this was not what I was looking for but other than that she didn't know of any place. As much as modern technology drives me crazy at times, Google sure does come in handy.

After searching the area, I found a local steakhouse called Tucsons and headed on over. It was a great place with ice cold beer, and I ordered a delicious ribeye with all the fixings and their homemade bread was delicious. So, with a full belly and 304 miles under my belt it was time to settle in for the night.

Day 19
Osage Beach, Missouri

Looking at my map when I got back to the room, I was looking for some alternative routes to places I had never been before. I had a couple of options from Salina, I could go north into Iowa and if I did that I was going to Clear Lake, Iowa where Buddy Holly died in a plane crash on February 3, 1959. They have a pretty cool memorial to Buddy there, or I was going to keep heading east towards Osage Beach in Missouri. This was another point where I wished I had headed north and could have still gone to Osage Beach, but for some reason I just didn't think it through. I made a stop at a great historical spot called Lone Jack which was platted in 1841 and has a Post Office in operation since 1839. There was a battle of the Civil War in 1862 in which Federal troops were defeated by the Confederate troops in a battle that raged for five hours on the main street. They have a small civil war museum located here right across the street from the Cave Hotel which is from 1855 and is part of the Battlefield along with 150 acres which is just like it was during the battle, the preservation society is trying to acquire the land to preserve this piece of history. Lone Jack is located just southeast of Independence, Missouri and I probably passed this way back in 2012 but didn't stop at that time. Going into Windsor on my way to Osage Beach I passed a really nice display dedicated to our country. I love seeing these kinds of things along the way.

Osage Beach is located at Lake Ozark and close to Lake of the Ozarks state park. Lake of the Ozarks is a large lake that was built in 1929 and stretches over 93 miles. I had no idea what to expect here so I decided to drive around checking things out and seeing what was available as far as hotels and restaurants. I made a stop at a BBQ place called Wobbly Boots for a cold beer and to just hang out. The bartender there was really nice and after a couple of beers I decided to go ahead and eat here and had some yummy ribs. She was telling me about a state park about 12 miles away but worth the trip if you like history. It is the Ha Ha Tonka State Park, which encompasses over 3,700 acres on an arm of the Lake of the Ozarks. One of its great sites is the ruins of the stone castle that was modeled after European castles from the 16th century. Construction of the castle began in 1905 by Robert Snyder who unfortunately died in a car accident in 1906 and the building was completed by his sons in the early 1920s and the family used it as a summer and weekend home. In the late 1930s it was used as a hotel but was destroyed by a fire in 1942. The state purchased the grounds and the ruins of the castle and turned it into a state park. You can't walk in the ruins as they have been deemed unsafe, but you can get some great pictures from different observation points. The park itself is a popular place for boating, fishing, and hiking with over fifteen miles of trails. It was a great place to visit, and I actually hiked a few of the trails to some of the natural bridges. I was glad the young lady had told me about this place, and it was a nice ride out to the ruins. Now I needed to find a place to stay for the night and I wanted a place with a view of the lake. As I was looking for a motel, I found a little bar called Whiskers which was a local biker bar and had a couple of bourbon and cokes before heading back out to find a room. I made a stop at the Grand Glaize which was right on the lake but was pretty pricey at 280.00 for a night so I said I would let them know. I did some more looking around but as it was off season lots of places were closed. Once again good old Google came through and I found a room at the same hotel for 120.00 Per night on Booking.com, I think when I came back it pissed the guy at the desk off and he ended up giving me a room with a view of the parking lot, oh well he should have given me a better rate to begin with. It was a nice hotel with lots of amenities but too bad due to Covid the restaurant was still closed; it would have been nice to hang out there with a great view of the lake and enjoy some beverages. Another day in the books and I am getting closer to home, but I still have a few great sights to see.

Day 20
Evansville, Indiana & Owenboro, Kentucky

Today's ride would take me toward St. Louis to Evansville, Indiana and eventually Owensboro, Kentucky. As I got close to St. Louis I decided not to go through the city as I have been here twice before, and I jumped off onto some side roads which took me to another little historical find. I found the Route 66 state park on the Meramec River at the site of what was the former town of Times Beach. The town had quite a history as extreme levels of dioxin were found here and the town was dismantled and decontaminated by the EPA. The cool part of this area is that it was part of the Mother Road, Route 66 and I was able to get some great pictures here especially of the old Route 66 bridge which is closed for safety reasons. Once again getting off the Interstates brought me to this neat piece of history.

Evansville, Indiana ended up having so much history though I initially came here to take pictures of the many places from the Rosanne television show. Evansville was one of the places my daughter had highlighted in the travel book she made for me and one of the first stops was Bosse field which was the baseball field where 'A league of Their Own' was filmed which had such stars as Tom Hanks, Madonna, and Geena Davis, which was about the women's All American Girls Professional Baseball League, formed during World War 2. While trying to find this field there was a little league field close by where Don Mattingly of the New York Yankees played on as a young boy. I wish the field was open so that you could get good pictures, but I rode around it getting the best photos I could. There was also a plaque here commemorating Bob Griese the Hall of Fame quarterback of the Miami Dolphins who was also from Evansville. After visiting these sights, I was off on a tour around the town to find the sights from Rosanne which were scattered around the area. There were three main sights, one of which was the front of the house used in the opening scenes, also the church that the family attended and the bar that Dan hung out at. It was really cool seeing these locations and they were immediately recognizable. Once I had found these locations, Ellen had told me about a local donut shop called The Donut Bank which luckily was right around the corner from the house location and I arrived there right before they were closing, the donuts weren't bad, but we have local places in Virginia Beach that are better but still a new experience.

Evansville is a city in southwest Indiana on the Ohio River and was incorporated in 1817, at one time in the early 1900s Evansville was one of the largest hardwood furniture manufacturing centers in the world with over forty-one factories. I had originally planned to stay in Evansville for the night but after riding around and as it was still early, I decided to head on towards Owensboro, Kentucky just a few miles down the Ohio River. The Ohio River was one of the major rivers in the growth of our country. It Stretches over 981 miles from where the Monongahela River and the Allegheny River come together at Pittsburgh to form the Ohio. I have crossed the Ohio many times from some of the great cities in America. Once I arrived in Owensboro, trying to find lodging became a little difficult and the first place I stopped was a rather large motel but when I walked in found that most of the rooms were closed for remodeling, they said, but I wondered about that so I decided to go through town to see what I could find. I ended up at a Motel 6 which was pretty run down but as it was getting late, I was ready to stop for the night, sometimes the cheaper motels are nice, but others not very well maintained. There was a cool hamburger place right next to the hotel called Freddy's Steakburgers which is like Steak and Shake. It is a coast-to-coast chain founded by two brothers and a friend in 2002 and named after Freddy Simon, a World War 2 veteran. They have over 380 locations in 33 states, and we have one here in Suffolk, Virginia. It was a pleasant treat, and the food was tasty. I was getting closer to home and only had a couple of more days to go, and I was debating whether to take a couple of more days and do some riding in Tennessee or the mountains of Virginia.

Day 21
Bristol Tennessee/Virginia

Leaving Owensboro, I headed south down the William Natcher Parkway towards Bowling Green and then east to Bristol. I had made a rest stop and was talking to my daughter, and she was telling me about a hotel in Bristol that her coworker had stayed at called The Sessions as in a music session. I did some google research and it looked like a great place to stay and I booked a room which turned out to be a fantastic decision. The Sessions is considered a boutique hotel owned by the Marriott chain and opened in June of 2020. The decor pays tribute to the history of the area which is recognized to be the place where Country music began. There are multiple historic buildings in the complex such as the Bristol Grocery Store and the 1922 Service Granary Mill. Each of the 70 rooms pays tribute to the 1927 Bristol sessions and has all types of music memorabilia, there is also a restaurant called Southern Craft which serves many local foods and craft beers. I must say the beds they have are one of the most comfortable I have ever slept in, what a great night's sleep. The hotel was in a great location and within walking distance of most of the tourist attractions and venues.

    I spent lots of time walking around taking pictures and reading all of the plaques around town, it was so cool walking down one side of the street and I was in Tennessee and then on the other side being in Virginia. There is a famous burger place here called the Burger Bar. The Burger Bar has been open since 1942 and is known as the last place country star Hank Williams senior stopped in 1952 before he died in the backseat of his car traveling to a concert. Going inside is like a time capsule of country music with lots of memorabilia and newspaper clippings all over the wall. The sign over State Street that says Tennessee and Virginia was about eight blocks from the hotel but while walking down there for pictures it gave me a chance to look around and take pictures. While looking around I stopped into State Street Brewing, which was a huge brewery and had some really good craft beers. It was also right across the street from a park where there is always live music being performed. There are a couple of places on State Street one called the Paramount that have top named performers there almost every weekend, as I was walking around, I saw where Sister Hazel was playing that night and I should have gone to see them as tickets were only $35 dollars. Sometimes, I really irritate myself, I mean I will take a twenty-two-day trip and spend thousands of dollars and then tighten up over $35 dollars. I went back to the Brewery for a couple more beers and listened to the band in the park that you could hear from the bar. There are lots of historical sites to visit in the area as Virginia and Tennessee were both major battlefields during the Civil War. If you like auto racing the Bristol Motor Speedway is one of the premier tracks in NASCAR and is one of the largest seating wise sporting venues in the world even though it is a short track but is like a deep bowl. It is a half mile track that has some of the most intense racing on the Circuit. There are also numerous caverns and museums in this area, and if you ride a motorcycle, you are not very far from highway 129 which is the Tail of the Dragon, one of the most well-known rides in the country. It has 381 curves in eleven miles and can be very challenging especially on weekends during the summer especially with the sport bike riders as they push the limits of safety and sometimes sanity riding this road. I have ridden the Dragon eleven times, so I did not ride it this time plus I was going to hit some of the sections of the Claw of the Dragon just north of Galax, Virginia. Bristol had been a fantastic unplanned stop and looking back I should have stayed an extra night, but I plan on coming back here maybe next year as Laura and I are planning on taking a car trip to Albuquerque New Mexico to see the Balloon Festival.

Day 22
Wytheville & Virginia Beach

I slept in a little later this morning as I was going to make some stops in Wytheville, Virginia and do some mountain riding. One of the places in Wytheville I was stopping at was going to be Skeeters hot dogs and as they didn't open till 11 am and it wasn't that far I got to lay in that damn comfortable bed a little longer. Once I got up, I went and took a few more pictures of things I had missed the day before. Bristol had turned out to be such a delightful place with so much history of all types from cultural to architecture, and sports. It was only about 70 miles from Bristol to Wytheville, so I had plenty of time to do some nice back roads riding and even more after I left Wytheville. Wytheville is a small town in southwestern Virginia and named after George Wythe, one of the signers of the Declaration of Independence. It has the nickname of Crossroads of the Blueridge. It is also the birthplace of Edith Wilson, second wife of President Woodrow Wilson which a hotel in town is named after her. Wytheville has a little bit of dark history to it as I guess lots of towns have if you dig far enough. In 1926 the last documented lynching of an African American man took place, and in 1950 the town had a small outbreak of Polio turn into an epidemic. Despite these episodes today's Wytheville is a great little town with some cool places to visit, this is another place my daughter Ellen had found for me to explore some of these sights. As I arrived in town about 10:30 I had some time to explore before lunch at Skeeters. One of the neat photo opportunities was a place called Wytheville Office Supply, which has a huge pencil outside the entrance to the store. The pencil was constructed in the 1960s and is about 30 foot long and looks just like a giant # 2 yellow pencil, and just down the street is a giant paint can that appears to be pouring its paint down onto the sidewalk. These are cool little sights to see when in small towns. Wytheville also has one of the more than 275 LOVE signs that are throughout the state of Virginia to go along with the slogan Virginia is for Lovers, it is like a scavenger hunt to try to find as many as possible as you travel around the state. After getting the pictures I was after it was time for lunch at Skeeters Hot Dogs, established in 1925 and is one of Virginia's oldest continually operating restaurants. It is like stepping back in time to go in here to grab a couple of chili dogs which are called red hots made by the Valleydale Company with their delicious homemade chili and if you like soups try their homemade chili beans. I love a good hotdog and Skeeters was right up there with some of the best I have had, and lots of people agree as they have sold over seven million dogs since they opened. The restaurant looks pretty much the same as it did in 1925 inside and out, definitely recommend a stop here if you are traveling through the area. About half a mile outside downtown Wytheville is one of America's smallest churches, it is a 12 x 16 building that seats about eight people and is really beautiful inside with a cool bell tower outside and some very nice gardens, definitely worth a stop and take the time to go inside it.

    My next stop was about 12 miles outside of town and was another spot my daughter had found for me to visit, which was Big Walker Lookout. Big Walker Lookout is located on Big Walker Mountain along with the BW Country Store which has been in business for 75 years. Climbing the 100-foot-tall tower gives you a fantastic view around the area. There is a small charge to climb to the top which is about 200 steps. At first, I was like do I want to climb this but after looking around the store I said heck I'm here I will just take my time and make it to the top and I am damn glad I did. From the top you get a great view looking down highway 621 and 52 as they wind off into the mountains. Getting to the tower put me on what is part of the Claw of the Dragon which along with the Back of the Dragon are two of the premier riding spots in Virginia. I plan on making a trip here sometime to spend a few days and do both loops. I had planned on stopping for the night in Roanoke and as I headed that way and kept getting closer to home I made the decision to just suck it up and finish the ride home, though I had planned to be gone till October 4th I had already messed up a couple of times and by now I was just ready to get on back home.

    The trip had been an amazing ride and getting to spend part of it with Laura and some old friends at the beginning was nice. I had been able to see some new National Parks and put another 7000 miles under my belt plus create stories for another chapter in my riding books. This was my first real long trip on my Spyder, and the bike performed and rode great, and I got lots of thumbs up and comments along the way. Taking these trips always restores my faith in people and this great country regardless of what so many people try to jam down our throats. Most people I have found are really good people and willing to help you out if needed and I always enjoy meeting and talking to new people and learning a little about their lives.

ACKNOWLEDGMENTS

I have been so blessed to continue to do one of the things I love the most, and that is to travel the country and explore new sights with the support of my family, friends, and especially my loving wife Laura. I hope that my adventures will inspire others to do the same. Don't let everyday life consume your thoughts and time and not enjoy the beauty that is all around you. Even if it is a simple day trip somewhere for lunch or a month-long trip across the country just get out and do it. Don't have regrets and say I was going to do that someday. Our time here is short and get out and enjoy it.

    I have had the honor to travel across this country with two of my good friends, John Barnett and Bill Maxwell. We made memories that will never be forgotten and hopefully remembered through my stories, and though life may throw some curves as we get older, I will always be proud to call these two travel buddies my friend.

    Stay Safe and Enjoy the Ride!

Follow:
Instagram: @lonely_road_photos
E-mail: beachvette79@aol.com

If you enjoyed this book, check out my first book titled
Two Wheels and Fresh Air: The Adventures of a Rider.
Available for purchase on Amazon.

www.ingramcontent.com/pod-product-compliance
Lightning Source LLC
Chambersburg PA
CBHW061258040426
42444CB00010B/2416